My United States

Hawai'i

JOANNE MATTERN

Children's Press®
An Imprint of Scholastic Inc.

Content Consultant
James Wolfinger, PhD, Associate Dean and Professor
College of Education, DePaul University, Chicago, Illinois

Library of Congress Cataloging-in-Publication Data
Names: Mattern, Joanne, 1963– author.
Title: Hawai'i / by Joanne Mattern.
Description: New York, NY : Children's Press, 2017. | Series: A true book | Includes bibliographical references and index.
Identifiers: LCCN 2017002482| ISBN 9780531252550 (library binding) | ISBN 9780531232859 (pbk.)
Subjects: LCSH: Hawaii—Juvenile literature.
Classification: LCC DU623.25 .M359 2017 | DDC 996.9—dc23
LC record available at https://lccn.loc.gov/2017002482

Photographs ©: cover: Cavataio Vince/Getty Images; back cover ribbon: AliceLiddelle/Getty Images; back cover bottom: mashuk/iStockphoto; 3 bottom: NielsVK/Alamy Images; 3 map: Jim McMahon; 4 top: OGGM/iStockphoto; 4 bottom: Dave Fleetham/age fotostock; 5 bottom: jhorrocks/iStockphoto; 5 top: schutzphoto/iStockphoto; 7 bottom: theartist312/iStockphoto; 7 center top: vuk8691/iStockphoto; 7 center bottom: 400tmax/iStockphoto; 7 top: RobertCravens/iStockphoto; 8-9: Kicka Witte/Design Pics/Getty Images; 11: Stock Connection/Superstock, Inc.; 12: NASA/Roger Ressmeyer/Corbis/VCG/Getty Images; 13: Adalberto Ríos Szalay/age fotostock; 14: Pacific Stock - Design Pics/Superstock, Inc.; 15: Vicki Jauron/Babylon and Beyond Photography/Getty Images; 16-17: jewhyte/iStockphoto; 19: Cathy Bussewitz/AP Images; 20: Tigatelu/iStockphoto; 22 left: YAY Media AS/Alamy Images; 22 right: Brothers Good/Shutterstock; 23 center left: Kevin Schafer/Minden Pictures; 23 bottom: Dave Fleetham/age fotostock; 23 center right: Roger Hall/Science Source; 23 top right: OGGM/iStockphoto; 23 top left: ronen/iStockphoto; 23 top center: jhorrocks/iStockphoto; 24-25: lilbusca/iStockphoto; 27: John Webber/The Granger Collection; 29: Art Archive/Superstock, Inc.; 30: John Webber/The Granger Collection; 31 center: Superstock, Inc.; 31 right: YAY Media AS/Alamy Images; 31 left: Sarin Images/The Granger Collection; 32: Paul Schutzer/Getty Images; 33: Sarin Images/The Granger Collection; 34-35: jhorrocks/iStockphoto; 36: schutzphoto/iStockphoto; 37: RandyJayBraun/iStockphoto; 38: Peter Skinner/Science Source; 39: The Honolulu Advertiser, Deborah Booker/AP Images; 40 inset: NorthStar203/iStockphoto; 40 bottom: PepitoPhotos/iStockphoto; 41: Doug Perrine/Minden Pictures; 42 top left: Underwood Archives/The Image Works; 42 bottom left: Scott J. Ferrell/Congressional Quarterly/Alamy Images; 42 top right: Granamour Weems Collection/Alamy ImagesAlamy Images; 42 center: Evan Agostini/Invision/AP Images; 42 bottom right: NASA; 43 top left: Pete Souza/The White House/The Image Works; 43 top right: Sthanlee Mirador/Sipa USA/Newscom; 43 center right: Nick Potts/ZUMA Press/Newscom; 43 center left: Jaguarps/Dreamstime; 43 bottom left: Scott A. Miller/ZUMA Press/Newscom; 43 bottom center: dpa picture alliance/Alamy Images; 43 bottom right: Birdie Thompson/SIPA/Newscom; 44 top: Justinreznick/iStockphoto; 44 bottom: cweimer4/iStockphoto; 45 top: Chad Ehlers/Media Bakery; 45 center: stockstudioX/iStockphoto; 45 bottom: Kicka Witte/Design Pics/Getty Images.

Maps by Map Hero, Inc.

No part of this publication may be reproduced in whole or in part, or stored in a retrieval system, or transmitted in any form or by any means, electronic, mechanical, photocopying, recording, or otherwise, without written permission of the publisher. For information regarding permission, write to Scholastic Inc., Attention: Permissions Department, 557 Broadway, New York, NY 10012.
© 2018 Scholastic Inc.

All rights reserved. Published in 2018 by Children's Press, an imprint of Scholastic Inc.
Printed in the United States of America 113

SCHOLASTIC, CHILDREN'S PRESS, A TRUE BOOK™, and associated logos are trademarks and/or registered trademarks of Scholastic Inc., 557 Broadway, New York, NY 10012.
1 2 3 4 5 6 7 8 9 10 R 27 26 25 24 23 22 21 20 19 18

Front cover: A team paddling an outrigger canoe near Oʻahu

Back cover: Plumeria flowers

Welcome to Hawai'i

Find the Truth!

Everything you are about to read is true *except* for one of the sentences on this page.

Which one is **TRUE**?

T or F Hawai'i is the only U.S. state made up of islands.

T or F Hawai'i became a state in 1900.

UNITED STATES

Hawai'i

HAWAII
ZBE 050
• ALOHA STATE •

Find the answers in this book.

Contents

1 Land and Wildlife

2 Government

THE BIG TRUTH!

Yellow hibiscus

What Represents Hawai'i?

Hawaiian triggerfish

Surfer in Hawai'i

Hula dancer

This Is Hawai'i!

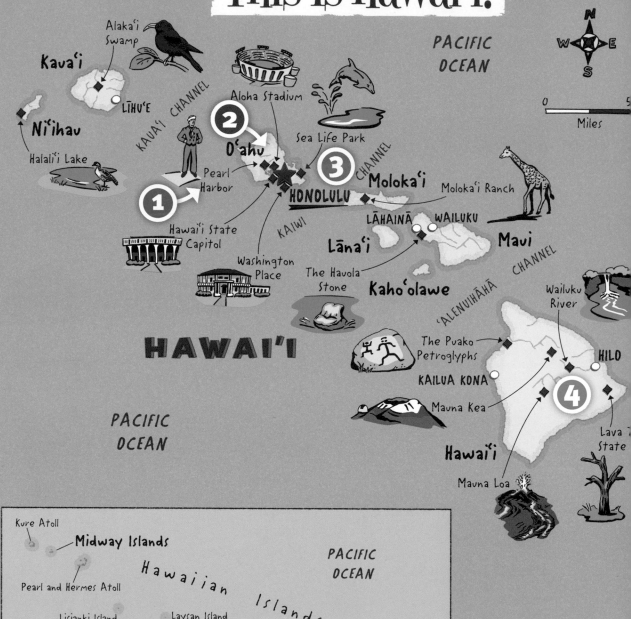

PACIFIC OCEAN

Kaua'i

Alaka'i Swamp

LĪHU'E

Ni'ihau

Halali'i Lake

KAUA'I CHANNEL

Aloha Stadium

2

O'ahu

Sea Life Park

1 → Pearl Harbor

Hawai'i State Capitol

Washington Place

KAIWI

3

HONOLULU

CHANNEL

Moloka'i

Moloka'i Ranch

LĀHAINĀ   WAILUKU

Lāna'i

The Havola Stone

Kaho'olawe

Maui

'ALENUIHĀHĀ   CHANNEL

HAWAI'I

The Puako Petroglyphs

KAILUA KONA

Mauna Kea

Mauna Loa

Hawai'i

Wailuku River

4

HILO

Lava State

PACIFIC OCEAN

N W E S

0   5
Miles

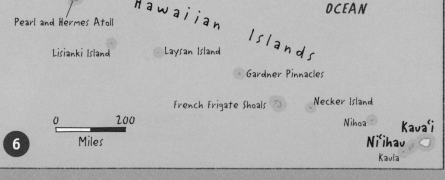

Kure Atoll

Midway Islands

Pearl and Hermes Atoll

Lisianki Island

Hawaiian Islands

Laysan Island

Gardner Pinnacles

French Frigate Shoals

Necker Island

Nihoa

PACIFIC OCEAN

Kaua'i

Ni'ihau

Kaula

0   200
Miles

6

① Pearl Harbor

This is where Japanese forces bombed the U.S. naval fleet in 1941, leading to U.S. involvement in World War II. Today, the site is a museum that honors the more than 2,000 Americans killed in the attack.

② O'ahu

O'ahu has the largest population of any of the Hawaiian Islands. About two-thirds of all Hawaiians live here.

③ Honolulu

This is Hawai'i's capital city. It is located on the island of O'ahu. This popular vacation destination features museums, theaters, sporting events, and the world-famous Waikiki Beach.

④ Hawai'i

This is the largest island in the state. Often called the Big Island, it is the home of Mauna Loa and Mauna Kea, two of the state's most incredible volcanoes.

The Big Island of Hawai'i was formed from five volcanoes.

CHAPTER 1

Land and Wildlife

Hawai'i, the 50th state, is unique in many ways. It's the only state that is not part of North America. It's the only state comprised entirely of islands—islands with tropical beaches, volcanoes, and snowy mountain peaks. There are 137 of them in the state. And Hawai'i is the only state where the same word—*aloha*—is used as both a greeting and a farewell!

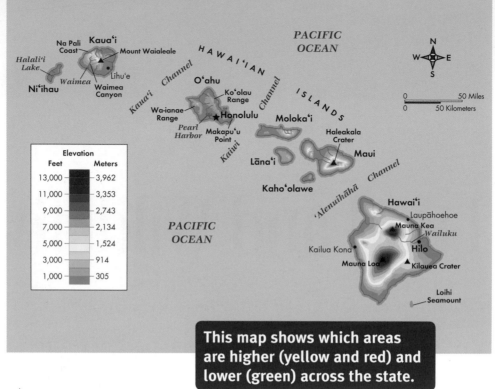

This map shows which areas are higher (yellow and red) and lower (green) across the state.

Geography

Millions of years ago, volcanoes **erupted** in the Pacific Ocean. These eruptions created the islands of Hawai'i. Some of these islands are large, and others are tiny. Together, they cover 10,931 square miles (28,311 square kilometers). The eight largest islands lie at the southeastern end of the **archipelago**. They are named Hawai'i, Kaho'olawe, Maui, Lāna'i, Moloka'i, O'ahu, Kaua'i, and Ni'ihau.

Mauna Loa and Kilauea

Some of Hawai'i's volcanoes are still active today. Mauna Loa is Hawai'i's most famous volcano. The last time it erupted was in 1984, but scientists are sure it will one day erupt again.

Kilauea (pictured) is the world's most active volcano. It is located near Mauna Loa on the Big Island. Both volcanoes can be seen in Hawai'i Volcanoes National Park.

Climate

Hawai'i has a mild climate. Temperatures are usually between 70 and 90 degrees Fahrenheit (21 and 32 degrees Celsius). The weather is warmer near sea level and cooler high in the mountains.

Sometimes the islands are hit with fierce storms. Tropical storms and hurricanes form in the Pacific Ocean and frequently travel north toward Hawai'i. The state's worst hurricane was Hurricane Iniki, which struck in 1992.

MAXIMUM
TEMPERATURE
100°F

MINIMUM
TEMPERATURE
12°F

Hurricane Iniki struck the island of Kaua'i with winds of 145 miles per hour (233 km per hour).

The tops of Hawai'i's tallest mountains are covered with snow during the winter.

Nani Mau Gardens on the Big Island has 22 acres (9 hectares) of rare tropical plants, including colorful orchids.

Plants

Hawai'i's warm climate means that many different plants can flourish there. Some of the most common ones are orchids, which produce beautiful and colorful flowers. Trees such as hala, magnolia, and plumeria also thrive on the islands. Many different species of ferns are found in Hawai'i as well.

Hawai'i has many fruit-producing plants. There are lychee, star apple, and mountain apple trees. Mangoes, papayas, strawberries, guavas, and passion fruit also grow wild all over the islands.

Spinner dolphins are a common sight near the shores of Hawai'i's islands.

Animals

Hawai'i is home to many **native** animal species. Because the state is made up of islands, many of these animals are not found anywhere else in the world. Colorful birds fly through the sky, and the waters are filled with fish, whales, dolphins, and seals. Amazingly, Hawai'i's only native land mammals are bats!

Uninvited Guests

Other animals were brought to Hawai'i from distant places when humans settled on the islands. Unfortunately, these species have often caused problems for the native animals. For example, rats came to the islands aboard ships. To get rid of the rats, people brought mongooses to the islands. However, the mongooses also ate bird eggs. Bird populations dropped while the mongoose population got bigger.

Today, it is illegal for people in Hawai'i to keep mongooses as pets or bring them into the state.

Honolulu is Hawaiian for "sheltered harbor."

CHAPTER 2

Government

Hawai'i's largest city, Honolulu, is also its capital. It has been the capital city since 1850, when the islands were still part of an independent kingdom. Hawai'i's state capitol is unlike any other in the nation. It was designed with a unique Hawaiian style. Inside, the main legislative chambers are even volcano-shaped!

Three Branches

Hawai'i's government is divided into three branches: executive, legislative, and judicial. Led by the governor, the executive branch is responsible for carrying out Hawai'i's state laws. Hawai'i's legislative branch is divided into two houses: a 25-member Senate and a 51-member House of Representatives. The legislature's most important job is to create new laws. The judicial branch of government includes all of Hawai'i's courts. The highest court in Hawai'i is the state's supreme court.

HAWAI'I'S STATE GOVERNMENT

LEGISLATIVE BRANCH
Writes and passes state laws

Senate (25 members)	House of Representatives (51 members)

EXECUTIVE BRANCH
Carries out state laws

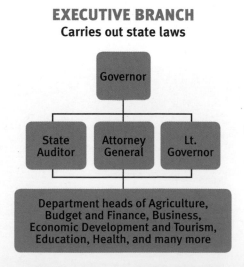

Governor

State Auditor	Attorney General	Lt. Governor

Department heads of Agriculture, Budget and Finance, Business, Economic Development and Tourism, Education, Health, and many more

JUDICIAL BRANCH
Enforces state laws

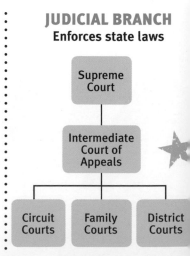

Supreme Court

Intermediate Court of Appeals

Circuit Courts	Family Courts	District Courts

Honolulu's mayor meets with local police to explain new laws to residents.

Hawai'i's Local Leaders

In most states, each town or city has its own local government. These governments collect taxes, set local laws, and oversee important services. But in Hawai'i, the only smaller governments below the state level are counties. People live on seven of Hawai'i's eight major islands. These seven islands are organized into just five counties. Each county governs the towns and cities in it.

Hawai'i in the National Government

Each state sends elected officials to represent it in the U.S. Congress. Like every state, Hawai'i has two senators. The U.S. House of Representatives relies on a state's population to determine its numbers. With its fairly small population, Hawai'i has just two representatives in the House.

Every four years, states vote on the next U.S. president. Each state is granted a number of electoral votes based on its members in Congress. With two senators and two representatives, Hawai'i has four electoral votes.

2 senators and 2 representatives

4 electoral votes

With four electoral votes, Hawai'i's voice in presidential elections is fairly small.

Representing Hawai'i

Elected officials in Hawai'i represent a population with a range of interests, lifestyles, and backgrounds.

Ethnicity (2015 estimates)

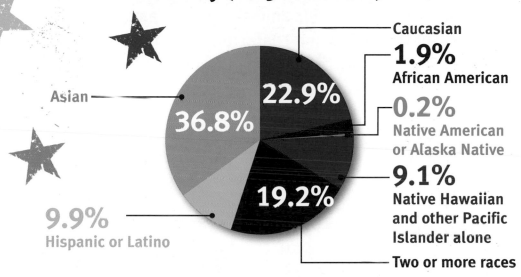

Caucasian
22.9%

1.9%
African American

0.2%
Native American or Alaska Native

Asian
36.8%

9.1%
Native Hawaiian and other Pacific Islander alone

19.2%
Two or more races

9.9%
Hispanic or Latino

31% of the population have a degree beyond high school.

92% live in cities.

57% own their own homes.

18% of Hawaiians were born in other countries.

91% of the population graduated from high school.

25% speak a language other than English at home.

What Represents Hawai'i?

States choose specific animals, plants, and objects to represent the values and characteristics of the land and its people. Find out why these symbols were chosen to represent Hawai'i or discover surprising curiosities about them.

Seal

Hawai'i's state seal shows King Kamehameha I on one side and the goddess of liberty on the other. The goddess is holding the Hawaiian flag. The number 1959 on the seal is the year Hawai'i became a state. The state motto is written in Hawaiian around the edge of the seal. In English, it means "The life of the land is perpetuated in righteousness."

Flag

The stripes on Hawai'i's state flag stand for the state's eight major islands. The British flag is in the upper left corner because the islands were once protected by Great Britain.

Ukulele

STATE MUSICAL INSTRUMENT

This four-stringed instrument was invented in Hawai'i in the 1800s.

Yellow Hibiscus

STATE FLOWER

Hibiscus flowers of many colors grow throughout Hawai'i. The yellow variety was chosen in 1988 to represent the state.

Nene

STATE BIRD

Also known as the Hawaiian goose, this bird is found only in Hawai'i.

Hula

STATE DANCE

Hula has been a part of Hawaiian culture since the earliest people settled on the islands centuries ago.

Kamehameha Butterfly

STATE INSECT

This insect is one of two butterfly species that does not live anywhere outside of Hawai'i.

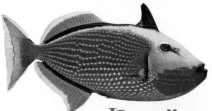

Hawaiian Triggerfish

STATE FISH

The Hawaiian name for this fish is *humuhumunukunukuāpua'a*.

The throne room in Honolulu's 'Iolani Palace during the 1800s

ALOHA

CHAPTER 3

History

People have lived in Hawai'i for more than 1,500 years. Many different groups of settlers have made their way to the islands. Each of these groups brought its own unique culture and traditions. Over the centuries, these different traditions have all become part of Hawai'i's rich culture.

Early People

The first people to settle in Hawai'i were probably sailors from Polynesia. They arrived during the third or fourth century CE. Hawaiians call these early settlers *ka poe kahiko*, which means "people of the past."

The ka poe kahiko settled on the islands and developed a new society. These early Hawaiians fished and hunted for food. They also grew crops such as bananas and coconuts.

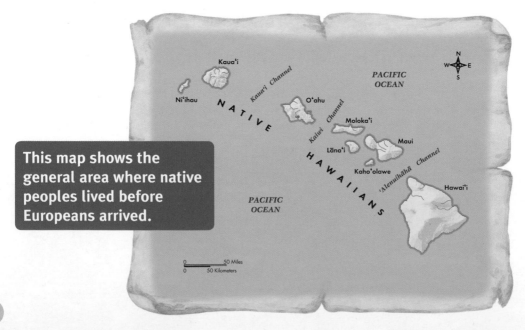

This map shows the general area where native peoples lived before Europeans arrived.

Native Hawaiians relied on handmade boats for fishing and traveling.

Native Hawaiians

Hawaiian society was divided into **castes**. The highest caste was the *ali'i*. The ali'i ruled with the help of kahunas, or priests. The middle caste was called the *maka'ainana*, or commoners. This caste included farmers, fishers, and craftspeople. Slaves and outcasts belonged to the lowest caste. Everyone followed strict rules depending on their caste. These rules were called *kapu*.

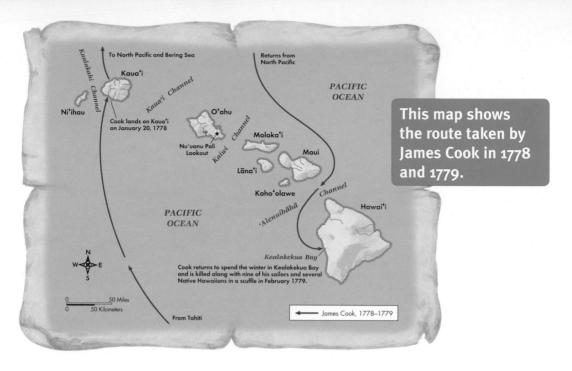

This map shows the route taken by James Cook in 1778 and 1779.

For many years, each island had its own ruler. Sometimes, these rulers and their people fought wars with each other. Things began to change in the 1780s. During that time, Kamehameha, the ruler of the island of Hawai'i, began to gather more power. In 1795, he conquered the islands of O'ahu, Maui, Lāna'i, and Moloka'i. By 1810, he was crowned Kamehameha I, the first king of all of Hawai'i. But things changed in even bigger ways as Europeans began arriving on the islands.

European Exploration

The first European to arrive was a British explorer named Captain James Cook. This was in 1778. At first, the natives welcomed the British. Then the British broke many kapu and did not respect local customs. In 1779, a group of Hawaiians killed Cook. However, Europeans continued to arrive. By the early 1800s, small groups of settlers from Great Britain, France, Russia, and the United States had come to live on the islands.

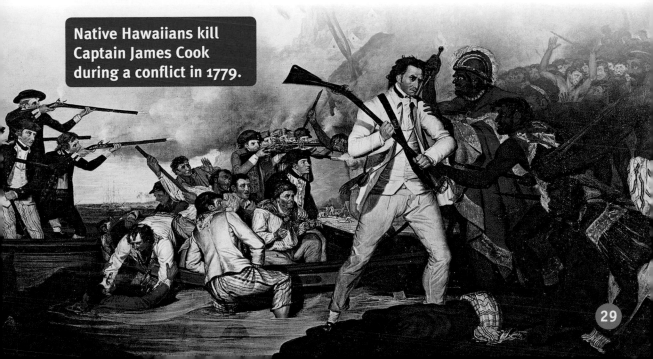

Native Hawaiians kill Captain James Cook during a conflict in 1779.

In 1835, an American named William Hooper came to Hawai'i and built the islands' first sugar **plantation**. Soon plantations growing pineapple and other crops sprang up across the islands. Hundreds of thousands of people from other countries came to Hawai'i to work. In addition, U.S. businesspeople began to get involved in Hawai'i's government.

Timeline of Hawai'i Events

1400s
Many fishing villages are established on the islands.

1778
British explorer Captain James Cook arrives in Hawai'i.

| 300 CE | 1400s | 1778 | 1810 |

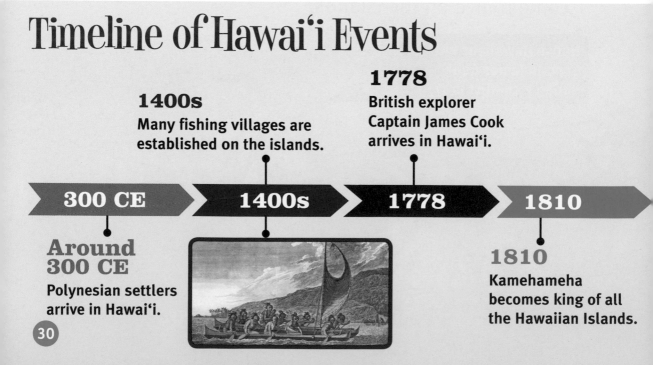

Around 300 CE
Polynesian settlers arrive in Hawai'i.

1810
Kamehameha becomes king of all the Hawaiian Islands.

War and Statehood

In 1900, Hawai'i became a U.S. **territory**. The United States built a naval base at Pearl Harbor on O'ahu. On December 7, 1941, Japanese planes bombed the base. This attack pushed the United States to declare war on Japan and enter World War II.

Many people wanted Hawai'i to become a state. Finally, their wishes came true on August 21, 1959.

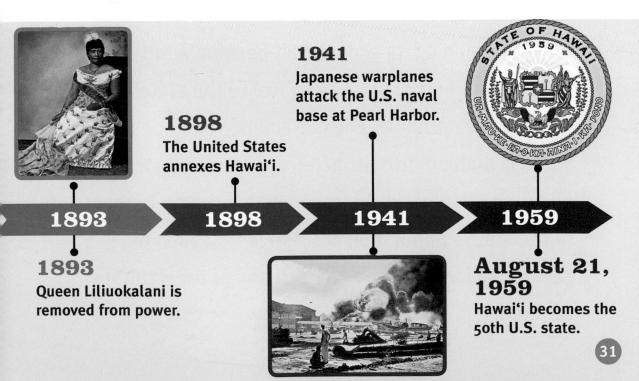

1941
Japanese warplanes attack the U.S. naval base at Pearl Harbor.

1898
The United States annexes Hawai'i.

| 1893 | 1898 | 1941 | 1959 |

1893
Queen Liliuokalani is removed from power.

August 21, 1959
Hawai'i becomes the 50th U.S. state.

Hawaiian senators and local leaders hold up the Hawaiian flag in celebration of winning statehood in 1959.

After it became a state, Hawai'i focused on strengthening its economy. It became a top destination for tourists, who travel to the state to enjoy its beautiful beaches, dramatic volcanoes, and warm climate. It also attracted new residents from all around the world. Today, an estimated 23 percent of the state's population are Native Hawaiian or part Hawaiian. Over the years, many of their cultural traditions have been lost.

Queen Liliuokalani

Lydia Kamakaeha was born in 1838. Her family was important in Hawaiian society, and her mother served as an adviser to King Kamehameha III. In 1874, Lydia's brother became king of the islands. In 1891, he died, and she became queen. The first woman ever to rule Hawai'i, she tried to make the **monarchy** stronger and reduce the influence of business in government. Instead, she was overthrown by a group of American businesspeople in 1893. After that, she fought against U.S. efforts to **annex** Hawai'i, but her efforts failed. She died in Hawai'i in 1917 at the age of 79.

33

Culture

Hawaiians love arts, sports, and food, and are happy to share their beautiful culture with others. Music and dance are important and popular parts of Hawaiian culture. The hula is a special dance that is accompanied by music played on drums and ukuleles. Dancers move their hands and bodies to tell a story.

Riding the Waves

Because Hawai'i is made up of islands, many of its most popular sports are enjoyed on the water. Surfing is an ancient Hawaiian sport. Native Hawaiians call it *he'e nalu*, or "wave sliding." Today, the sport is popular all over the world. Many Hawaiians also enjoy boating. Other favorite water sports are swimming, scuba diving, and fishing.

Surfing was invented by the Polynesian people who settled Hawai'i centuries ago.

Hawaiian Holidays

Hawai'i has many celebrations you won't find anywhere else. Each May 1, the entire state celebrates Lei Day, a holiday honoring the traditional Hawaiian craft of making floral wreaths to be worn

Leis are often made using fresh, locally grown flowers.

around the neck. On June 11, Hawai'i celebrates Kamehameha Day in honor of the king who united the islands. The state also holds annual surfing competitions, coffee festivals, and more.

Hawaiians at Work

Hawaiians work in many different occupations. Service industries employ the most people. Hotels, stores, restaurants, banks, and other businesses employ thousands of people. Tourism provides many jobs for Hawaiians.

About one-third of Hawai'i's land is used for farming. Sugar and pineapples are important crops. Fruit canning and other manufacturing also provide many jobs.

A huge farm in Kaua'i grows taro, a root vegetable often used in traditional Hawaiian cuisine.

Changing Technologies, Changing Jobs

A growing number of Hawaiians work in technology. In 2015, the state government began a $30 million program to attract more technology companies to the islands. The government hopes the program will help provide about 80,000 new jobs to the state's residents. The state is also looking to use technology to provide cleaner sources of energy.

Hawaiian business person Dustin Shindo (left) speaks with Representative John Karamatsu (right) at the opening of a new technology company in Hawai'i.

39

Good Food

The people of Hawai'i love fresh, delicious food. A Hawaiian feast is called a luau. Luaus feature many different traditional foods, including pineapple, mangoes, and fish. Poi is another popular food. Poi is a thick paste made from taro root that is scooped up with the fingers. No luau would be complete without a pig that has been slow-cooked in a pit oven.

 ## Haupia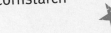

Ask an adult to help you!

Try this delicious Hawaiian coconut pudding. You can enjoy it either warm or chilled.

Ingredients
6 tablespoons sugar
5 tablespoons cornstarch

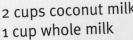

2 cups coconut milk
1 cup whole milk

Directions
Mix the sugar and cornstarch in a bowl. Add half the coconut milk and heat the mixture in a saucepan over low heat. While stirring, slowly add the whole milk and the other half of the coconut milk. The pudding will thicken as you stir. Sprinkle with shaved coconut (optional), serve, and enjoy!

A scuba diver encounters raccoon butterfly fish off the coast of the Big Island's Kona area.

Hawai'i is a special part of the United States. It has a long history that is very different from other parts of the nation. With its ancient traditions, beautiful islands, and friendly people, Hawai'i adds a tropical flavor to America's story. ★

Famous People

Duke Kahanamoku

(1890–1968) was a swimmer and surfer known as the Human Fish. He won gold medals in swimming at the 1912 and 1920 Olympics. He is also considered the father of modern surfing and helped make the sport popular around the world.

Don Ho

(1930–2007) was born in Honolulu and grew up on Oʻahu. He became a popular singer, comedian, and storyteller and helped introduce Hawaiian culture to people all over the world.

Daniel K. Inouye

(1924–2012) was born in Honolulu. He became Hawaiʻi's first representative in Congress and the nation's first Japanese American congressperson. He served eight terms in the U.S. Senate.

Lois Lowry

(1937–) is a popular children's author. She was born in Honolulu while her father was stationed there in the army. Lowry's books include *Number the Stars*, *The Giver*, and the *Anastasia Krupnik* series.

Ellison Onizuka

(1946–1986) was Hawaiʻi's first astronaut. He was born in Kealakekua on the island of Hawaiʻi. He became the first Asian American in space when he joined the crew of the space shuttle *Discovery* in 1985.

Barack Obama

(1961–) was the first African American president of the United States. He was born in Honolulu and lived in Hawai'i for much of his childhood.

Carrie Ann Inaba

(1968–) was born in Honolulu and became a dancer, singer, and choreographer. She is best known as a judge on the popular TV show *Dancing With the Stars*.

Bethany Hamilton-Dirks

(1990–) lost her left arm in a shark attack while surfing in her native Hawai'i as a teenager. She went on to become a professional surfer.

Michelle Wie

(1989–), who grew up in Honolulu, began playing golf when she was four years old. She became a professional golfer when she was just 15 and continues to play on the professional tour.

Manti Te'o

(1991–) was born and raised in Hawai'i. He was a star football player in high school and college, and went on to play for the San Diego Chargers and New Orleans Saints.

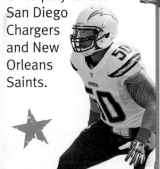

Kyla Ross

(1996–) was part of the U.S. gymnastics team at the 2012 Olympics, where she helped the team win a gold medal. She was born in Honolulu.

Auli'i Cravalho

(2000–) is an actress and singer who was born and raised in Hawai'i. She gained worldwide fame as the voice of the title character in the Disney movie *Moana*.

Did You Know That ...

Hawai'i's highest point is the peak of Mauna Kea at 13,796 feet (4,205 meters) above sea level. If you count the part of Mauna Kea that is underwater, the mountain is more than 33,000 feet (10,058 m) tall. This makes it the tallest mountain on earth!

The combined land of the Hawaiian Islands could fit inside Texas 24 times!

Texas is 24 times bigger than HI.

Hawai'i has two official languages: English and Hawaiian. The Hawaiian language has been used by Native Hawaiians since they first settled in the islands long ago.

There are more than 7,000 farms in Hawai'i.

Nearly 9 million tourists visit Hawai'i every year.

About 20 percent of Hawai'i is national park land.

Did you find the truth?

T Hawai'i is the only U.S. state made up of islands.

F Hawai'i became a state in 1900.

Resources

Books

Nonfiction

Benoit, Peter. *The Attack on Pearl Harbor*. New York: Children's Press, 2013.

Kent, Deborah. *Hawai'i*. New York: Children's Press, 2014.

Fiction

Mazer, Harry. *A Boy at War: A Novel of Pearl Harbor*. New York: Aladdin Paperbacks, 2002.

White, Ellen Emerson. *Kaiulani: The People's Princess*. New York: Scholastic, 2001.

Yamanaka, Louis-Ann. *Name Me Nobody*. New York: Hyperion, 1999.

Movies

Blue Hawai'i (1961)

From Here to Eternity (1953)

Lilo & Stitch (2002)

Moana (2016)

Soul Surfer (2011)

Tora! Tora! Tora! (1970)

Visit this Scholastic website for more information on Hawai'i:

★ www.factsfornow.scholastic.com
Enter the keyword **Hawai'i**

Important Words

aloha (uh-LOH-ha) a Hawaiian word meaning both "hello" and "goodbye"

annex (AN-eks) take control of a country or territory

archipelago (ar-kuh-PEL-uh-goh) a group of islands

castes (KASTS) strict social classes

erupted (i-RUP-tid) suddenly and violently threw out lava, hot ashes, and steam

monarchy (MAH-nur-kee) a government ruled by a king or queen

native (NAY-tiv) describing an animal or plant that lives or grows naturally in a certain place, or relating to the people who were originally in a place

plantation (plan-TAY-shuhn) a large farm found in warm climates where crops such as coffee, rubber, and cotton are grown

territory (TER-uh-tor-ee) an area connected with or owned by a country that is outside the country's main borders

Index

Page numbers in **bold** indicate illustrations.

About the Author

Joanne Mattern has written more than 250 books for children. She especially likes writing about all the fascinating places in our world. Joanne also loves American history and thinks we are a very interesting nation! She grew up in New York State and still lives there with her husband, four children, and several pets.